MW00892360

J.D VANCE

THE INCREDIBLE STORY OF

The Hillbilly Elegy

Author and His Journey to Fame

M.P KRUGER

Copyright 2024, by M.P Kruger

No part of this publication may be reproduced, distributed, or transmitted in any form or by any means, including photocopying without the prior written permission of the publisher, except in the case of brief quotations embodied in critical reviews and certain other noncommercial uses permitted by copyright law.

This work is dedicated to all the phoenixes who rise from the ashes of life to carve a great future for themselves.

Contents

Introduction

He is a Christian, a lawyer, a senator, an author of a bestselling book, a proud husband, and a former United States Marine. He is a phoenix for he arose from the ashes of obscurity and poverty to carve a life his younger self never dreamed possible. He is James David Vance, the one whom Donald Trump had chosen to be his vice-presidential running mate in the November 2024 election. The man who would help the Republicans achieve their conservative goals and reshape the future of America.

He now sings Trump's praises, but he was once his arch-enemy, and hated everything about him, calling him an obnoxious, reprehensible, and cynical asshole who was nothing short of a cultural heroin. To some, Vance is fickle, an opportunist, a chameleon, and a puppet in the hands of billionaires like Peter Thiel, whereas others see him as a genius who beat every odd to stay in the forefront of American politics.

In this book, I will tell the story of J.D Vance: his early years, his struggles, his successes, his political ideologies, and how he came to be Trump's right-hand man. This is why I will take you to the Beginning.

The Beginning

J.D. Vance was born James Donald Bowman on 2nd August 1984, in Middletown, Ohio. He came into the world the same day that Jeff Blatnick became the first American to win a gold medal in Greco-Roman wrestling at the Los Angeles Olympics. Jeff was in remission from Hodgkin's disease, but like phoenixes do, he arose beyond his limitations.

Middletown was a town in transition when Vance was born. The town was once a thriving industrial hub where people from across the United States moved in their droves.

The steel belt was behind this move and the economic boom associated with the region. The peak of this came in the early 1940s when World War II caused the American steel industry to operate at over 100% of its capacity.

The entry of the United States into WWII created an unprecedented demand for steel which was needed in building military equipment. It was during this time that Vance's grandparents, James and Bonnie Vance, moved from Jackson, Kentucky, to Middletown, Ohio, looking for a better life. They were teenagers, Bonnie was 13 and pregnant while James was 16.

James started working at Armco Steel which was later renamed AK Steel. This company actively recruited workers from the economically depressed regions of Eastern Kentucky, where Vance's family originated.

The recruitment efforts were part of a broader trend known as the "Hillbilly Highway," where many families migrated from rural Appalachia to urban industrial centers in search of jobs and a better quality of life.

Appalachia, a region steeped in history and cultural significance, is situated in the central and southern sections of the Appalachian Mountains in the eastern United States. Its geographical boundaries extend from the western Catskill Mountains in New York, traversing Pennsylvania, and continuing through the Blue Ridge and Great Smoky Mountains down to northern Georgia, Alabama, and Mississippi. Notably, West Virginia is unique as it is the only state entirely encompassed within the Appalachian region.

As of 2021, Appalachia was home to approximately 26.3 million residents, with a demographic composition that is predominantly white, accounting for around 80% of the population. This diverse region encompasses 423 counties across 13 states, covering an expansive area of 206,000 square miles.

The rich history of Appalachia includes the presence of Native American hunter-gatherers who first arrived over 16,000 years ago, with archaeological sites like the Meadowcroft Rockshelter in Pennsylvania providing evidence of early human habitation. Scotch-Irish, German, and English immigrants arrived in the 1700s and left a distinct heritage and culinary tradition in southern Appalachia.

Hardship in Middletown

In the 1980s, Armco Steel downsized significantly due to the collapse of the American steel industry. This led to high unemployment and economic hardship for Appalachians and other residents of Middletown, with many of them struggling to put food on their tables.

It was in this bleak economic climate that Vance was born, a time when families suffered, and single mothers languished in abject poverty. This was a time when giving birth to children was easy, but taking care of them was not, and Vance's mother, Beverly, had two to care for as she had given birth to another child, Lindsay, in 1979 when she was 19, five years before Vance was born.

When Vance was born, his biological father, Donald Bowman, was an integral part of the family. Vance was named James Donald Bowman, taking part of his father's names. Sadly, when he was six, Donald worked out on the family– leaving Beverly with the two children to care for.

Beverly had two major problems: unstable relationships and drug addiction. She was married five times. It was her third husband, Bob Hamel, that adopted Vance and changed his name to James David Hamel. However, after the couple split, the name "Hamel" was replaced with "Vance."

Vance has recounted countless times that he never had a good childhood. His mother battled with addiction. She worked as a nurse, and had access to some prescription painkillers which she started taking herself. As her addiction got worse she switched to taking heroin.

With her drug use came physical and psychological abuse of her children. Things got so out of hand that one time she threatened to intentionally crash her car when she was riding with Vance. After this car incident, Vance and his sister Lindsay were placed under the care of their maternal grandparents whom they fondly called Papaw and Mamaw.

Scottish Descent

Like Donald Trump, J.D Vance has a strong Scottish descent. His Scottish origin is specifically linked to the Scots-Irish heritage. His parents, Donald Bowman and Beverly Vance, both come from this lineage. The Scots-Irish, often referred to as Ulster Scots, migrated to America in significant numbers during the 18th and 19th centuries, bringing with them their cultural traditions and values.

To be more specific, the surname "Vance" is of Scottish origin, derived from the old English word "fenn," meaning marshland. It is also connected to the Norman settlers of the *de Vaux clan*, who settled in Scotland after the Norman Conquest of England in 1066. The Vance family historically lived in East Lothian, Scotland, and their name reflects their ancestry from the Vaux or Vallibus region in Normandy.

Papaw and Mamaw, who were strong Democrats, played a major role in raising Vance and his elder sister, Lindsay. Papaw died in 1997 at the age of 68 while Mamaw passed away in 2005 at the age of 72.

Vance in the US. Marine Corps

There are many reasons people join the military: for some, it gives them a sense of patriotism; for others, the steady income and paychecks give them job security, whereas some others just want to go with the flow—doing what their peers do. According to Vance, his primary motivation for enlisting was to prepare him for adulthood.

In 2003, at the age of 19, Vance enlisted in the United States Marine Corps shortly after graduating from high school. His service coincided with Operation Iraqi Freedom (OIF) launched on March 20, 2003, to overthrow Iraqi dictator Saddam Hussein, who was found in violation of United Nations Security Council Resolutions(UNSCRs) regarding weapons of mass destruction (WMDs), particularly Resolution 1441, which was adopted on November 8, 2002.

Iraq was required to allow international weapons inspectors to oversee the destruction of its weapons of mass destruction and to provide full disclosure of its WMD programs. However, Iraq did not fully comply with these requirements, leading to claims of material breach of Resolution 687, which had mandated disarmament following the Gulf War.

Iraq repeatedly obstructed the work of United Nations Special Commission (UNSCOM) inspectors. This included denying access to certain sites, intimidating inspectors, and failing to provide necessary documentation.

Despite the resolutions, Iraq was alleged to have continued developing chemical, biological, and nuclear weapons, as well as long-range missiles, which were prohibited under the terms of various UNSCRs. The United States under the leadership of President George W. Bush launched the operation to put an end to Hussein's autocracy.

Vance served as a Combat correspondent in Iraq for a period of six months beginning in late 2005, shortly after his grandmother's death.

As a combat correspondent, his responsibilities included writing articles, taking photographs, and escorting civilian news reporters. His role allowed him to capture the daily lives of Marines and share their stories.

To crown his service, Vance was adorned with some notable awards such as the Navy and Marine Corps Achievement Medal, Marine Corps

Good Conduct Medal, Sea Service Deployment Ribbon, and Iraq Campaign Medal.

Vance's experience serving in the Iraq War significantly shaped his political views. After his deployment, he concluded that the Iraq War was an ill-advised and costly overseas entanglement with negative consequences. He now sees unsettling similarities between the run-up to the Iraq War and the calls for more U.S. support for Ukraine against Russian invasion.

In recent times Vance has compared U.S. involvement in Ukraine to the Iraq War, arguing against continuing to provide billions in aid to Ukraine and instead focusing on countering China's global power. He believes the "domino theory" of politics that was used to justify the Vietnam War also applied to Iraq and now Ukraine. In a 2024 speech, Vance said that in 2003, he made the mistake of supporting the Iraq War but that he later realized that he had been lied to.

Vance After the Marine Corps

After completing his service in the Marine Corps in 2007, Vance proceeded to study political science and philosophy at the Ohio State University taking advantage of the G.I. Bill's tuition benefits which significantly reduces tuition fees for veterans by providing various educational benefits. He graduated summa cum laude in 2009, with a Bachelor of Arts degree in political science and philosophy before pursuing a law degree at Yale Law School.

In 2010, Vance enrolled at Yale Law School, where he received a nearly full-ride scholarship. His time at Yale was transformative; he graduated in 2013 with a Juris Doctor degree.

During law school, he was encouraged by Professor Amy Chua, a faculty member at Yale Law School, to write about his upbringing, leading to the publication of *Hillbilly Elegy* in 2016. This memoir gained significant attention, becoming a bestseller and later a Netflix film, which further propelled Vance into the public eye.

At Yale, Vance also served as an editor for *The Yale Law Journal* and made important connections that would later facilitate his entry into the world of venture capital and politics. His experiences at Yale were complex; while he appreciated the opportunities it provided, he often felt like an outsider in the predominantly liberal environment, which he later criticized as being out of touch with conservative values.

A Little Touch of Politics

His first transition into the political arena began when he took on the role of legislative aide for Republican Senator John Cornyn of Texas during the Summer of 2011. This position was pivotal in shaping his understanding of the politics and the intricacies of governance. Serving as an aide to a prominent senator provided Vance with a front-row seat to the legislative process, allowing him to observe firsthand how laws are crafted, debated, and enacted.

During his time with Senator Cornyn, Vance was involved in various aspects of policy development and legislative strategy. This role required him to assist in drafting legislation, conducting research, and analyzing the implications of proposed bills. Working closely with seasoned lawmakers and their staff, Vance gained insights into the complexities of bipartisan negotiations and the often contentious nature of political discourse.

This experience was crucial for Vance, as it deepened his understanding of the mechanisms that drive government and the importance of building coalitions to advance legislative goals. Cornyn also had a good record in the legal system having served as Texas attorney general and a justice on the Texas Supreme Court being in the senate.

Vance's time in Cornyn's office also exposed him to the broader political ecosystem, including the influence of lobbyists, interest groups, and constituents. He learned how public opinion can shape policy decisions and how effective communication is essential for garnering support for initiatives. This knowledge would later inform his approach as a public figure, where he would need to navigate the delicate balance between representing his constituents and aligning with party leadership.

Vance's legislative role was not just about learning the ropes of politics; it was also about building a network of relationships that would prove invaluable in his future endeavors. The connections he made while working for Cornyn later opened doors to various opportunities. Fast forward more than a decade later in July 2024, Cornyn was at the National Republican Convention to affirm his support of Vance as the best fit for the Republican vice president position. He said Vance was smart and incredibly well spoken.

After graduating from Yale Law School in 2013 Vance began his career by clerking for Judge David Bunning in the U.S. District Court for the Eastern District of Kentucky. Bunning, who was appointed to the federal bench by President George W. Bush in 2002, is known for several notable rulings, including ordering a county clerk to jail for refusing to issue same-sex marriage licenses in 2015. Vance's role as a clerk was significant as it allowed him to gain firsthand experience in the judicial system, providing insights into legal processes and court operations.

His boss, Judge David Bunning, unlike Vance, came from a privileged background. Bunning's dad, Jim Bunning was a former Republican senator, and a Hall of Fame baseball star who served in the United States senate for a period of twelve years, 1999 to 2011. As a clerk, Vance assisted Bunning with legal research, drafting opinions, and navigating court procedures and operations. Clerkships are highly sought-after positions for recent law graduates, as they provide valuable mentorship from experienced judges and open doors to influential professional networks.

The Eastern District of Kentucky, where Bunning presides, encompasses 67 counties. As a clerk,

Vance gained insights into the legal issues and cases specific to this region, which would expand his understanding of the challenges facing working-class communities in Appalachia and the Rust Belt, a theme he would later explore in his bestselling memoir *Hillbilly Elegy.*

Vance at Sidley Austin LLP

After completing his brief clerkship with Judge David Bunning, Vance took a significant step in his legal career by joining Sidley Austin LLP, one of the largest and most prestigious law firms in the United States. Located in the heart of Chicago, Sidley Austin has a storied history that dates back to 1866, when it was founded as a small firm in a rapidly growing commercial hub. This environment was not merely a backdrop for Vance's early career; it was a crucible that would shape his professional identity and future ambitions.

At Sidley Austin, Vance immersed himself in corporate law, a field that required him to engage with complex legal issues and navigate high-stakes negotiations. The firm was known for its rigorous standards and demanding work culture, which pushed Vance to hone his legal skills in a fast-paced environment. He quickly learned the intricacies of business law, from mergers and acquisitions to compliance and regulatory matters. This experience was crucial, as it equipped him with the analytical tools and strategic thinking necessary for success in the legal world.

The firm's historical significance added another layer to Vance's experience. Sidley Austin has been involved in landmark cases and has represented some of the most influential corporations in America. Its legacy includes a commitment to excellence that has shaped the careers of many prominent lawyers. For Vance, working at such a distinguished firm was both an honor and a challenge. He found himself in the company of seasoned professionals who had navigated the complexities of the legal system and had made their mark on the industry.

One of the most transformative aspects of Vance's time at Sidley Austin was the opportunity to engage in high-stakes negotiations. He participated in discussions that could determine the fate of major corporations, learning the importance of persuasive communication and strategic decision-making.

These experiences were not just about winning cases; they were about understanding the broader implications of legal decisions on businesses and communities. Vance's ability to navigate these negotiations would later inform his approach to politics and public policy, where he would advocate for the interests of his constituents.

Moreover, Vance's tenure at Sidley Austin allowed him to build a robust professional network that would prove invaluable in his future endeavors. The connections he made with influential clients and colleagues opened doors to opportunities in venture capital and beyond. As he moved into the world of investment, the relationships he cultivated at Sidley became crucial assets, providing him with insights and support as he transitioned from law to business.

Despite the demanding nature of corporate law, Vance's time at Sidley Austin was not just about professional development; it was also a period of personal growth. He grappled with the complexities of his identity as a working-class individual navigating the elite corridors of power. This tension would later manifest in his writing, particularly in his bestselling memoir, *Hillbilly Elegy*, where he explored issues of class, identity, and the struggles of the white working class in America.

The World of Venture Capital

Peter Thiel is often portrayed as a maverick and contrarian in the venture capital world. Some consider him the king maker in Silicon valley, and now in politics. His relationship with Vance goes back to the early 2010s.

Vance first encountered Thiel in Yale Law School in 2011 when he came to give a talk. According to Vance, Thiel was "possibly the smartest person" he had ever spoken to. Their relationship blossomed from there with Thiel acting as his mentor.

Another aspect of his life that Thiel influenced greatly was his Christian faith. Before speaking with Thiel, Vance had a preconceived notion that only dumb people were Christians whereas the smart ones were atheists. Thiel was a Christian, and very smart, defying Vance's perception of Christians, and in 2019 he was baptized and welcomed into the Catholic faith.

In 2015, J.D. Vance made a significant career shift from the legal field to the world of venture capital by joining Mithril Capital, a firm co-founded by Peter Thiel. According to the report on Crunchbase Mithril

Capital invests in the macroeconomics, technology, and finance sectors.

This transition marked a pivotal moment in Vance's professional journey, allowing him to go deep into the ever changing ecosystem of technology startups and innovative companies. As a principal at Mithril, Vance focused on evaluating business models, conducting due diligence, and supporting portfolio companies in their growth strategies.

Mithril Capital was established with the vision of investing in companies that could drive transformative change across various sectors. Under Thiel's guidance, the firm sought to identify and nurture startups that demonstrated the potential for substantial impact.

Vance's role at Mithril involved not only assessing the viability of investment opportunities but also providing strategic support to help these companies navigate the challenges of scaling their operations. This experience was instrumental in enhancing Vance's business acumen, as he learned the intricacies of the tech industry and the factors that contribute to a startup's success.

Working alongside Thiel and other seasoned investors, Vance gained access to a network of influential figures in Silicon Valley. These connections would prove invaluable as he navigated his subsequent ventures and political aspirations. Thiel, known for his role as a co-founder of PayPal and an early investor in Facebook, was a powerful ally in the tech world. His endorsement and support would later play a crucial role in Vance's political ascent, particularly as he sought to align himself with the Republican Party's evolving dynamics.

While Vance's tenure at Mithril Capital was relatively short, lasting until sometime in 2017. However, he was still working with Mithril when he published *Hillbilly Elegy: A Memoir of a Family and Culture in Crisis*. Vance's memoir gained significant traction after its publication in 2016. Written while he was still at Yale Law School, the book resonated deeply with many readers, becoming a bestseller and sparking widespread discussion about the socio-economic issues facing rural America.

Hillbilly Elegy offers a poignant narrative about Vance's upbringing in working-class Ohio, detailing the struggles and triumphs of his family, who were rooted in Appalachian culture. The memoir recounts his grandparents' journey from poverty in Kentucky to the hope of a better life in Ohio, yet it also delves into the challenges that plagued their family, including addiction, economic hardship, and familial instability. Vance's candid exploration of these themes struck a chord with readers, as it provided a personal lens through which to view the broader decline of the white working class in America.

The success of *Hillbilly Elegy* propelled Vance into the public eye, leading to numerous speaking engagements at universities and conferences. As he spoke about his experiences and the challenges faced by the working class, he became a sought-after commentator on issues of class, culture, and politics. His ability to articulate the struggles of his upbringing allowed him to connect with diverse audiences, from conservatives who resonated with his values of personal responsibility to liberals who were concerned about the systemic issues facing rural communities.

Vance's public speaking engagements often focused on the themes present in his memoir, such as the importance of family, the impact of socio-economic conditions on individual lives, and the cultural values that shape communities. He discussed the complexities of identity and the challenges of upward mobility, drawing from his own life story to illustrate the broader societal issues at play. His narrative not only highlighted the personal struggles he faced but also served as a critique of the societal structures that contribute to the disintegration of communities like his own.

The book's popularity also coincided with a growing interest in the political landscape of rural America, particularly in the wake of the 2016 presidential election. Vance's insights into the cultural and economic factors that influenced the political shift in Appalachia resonated with many who were trying to understand the dynamics of the electorate. His commentary on the region's transition from a strong Democratic base to a Republican stronghold provided a framework for discussing the broader implications of class and culture in American politics.

However, the book was not without its critics. Some argued that Vance's portrayal of Appalachia and its people reinforced negative stereotypes, oversimplifying complex social issues and failing to account for systemic factors contributing to poverty and dislocation. Critics pointed out that while Vance's personal narrative was compelling, it risked generalizing the experiences of an entire region based on his individual story. This backlash led to the publication of responses, such as *Appalachian Reckoning: A Region Responds to Hillbilly Elegy*, which aimed to provide a broader perspective on the issues Vance addressed.

Despite the mixed reviews, *Hillbilly Elegy* solidified Vance's reputation as an author and public intellectual. The memoir's impact extended beyond literature; it became a cultural touchstone that sparked conversations about class, identity, and the American dream. As Vance transitioned into politics, the themes explored in his book continued to inform his narrative and political strategy.

The success of the memoir not only established Vance as a prominent voice on issues affecting the working class but also solidified his reputation as a thought leader within conservative circles. His experiences in venture capital and the insights gained from working with innovative companies informed the narratives he presented in his writing and public speaking engagements.

After his stint at Mithril, Vance continued to explore opportunities in venture capital, eventually joining

Revolution, a Washington D.C based investment firm co-founded by former AOL CEO Steve Case.

Vance and The AOL Pioneer

Steve Case, co-founder of America Online (AOL), is a prominent figure in the tech industry and venture capital world. After leading AOL to become one of the largest internet service providers in the 1990s, Case transitioned into venture capital, establishing Revolution in 2005, a firm focused on investing in startups outside of Silicon Valley. His initiative, "Rise of the Rest," aims to support entrepreneurs in underserved regions across the United States, with the goal of enhancing economic growth and innovation beyond the traditional tech hubs.

According to the firm's report, California, New York, and Massachusetts accounted for about 75% of all the venture capital funding between 2014 and 2016.

Case's vision is rooted in the belief that the next wave of innovation will come from diverse locations and industries. He has been an advocate for investing in local economies and empowering founders who are addressing critical challenges in their communities. His work reflects a commitment to fostering entrepreneurship and creating opportunities for growth in the American economy.

When Case read Hillbilly Elegy, and knew that the author was a venture capitalist in Silicon Valley, he believed he had met the one that would help him in reaching the underserved regions of the United States. The focus of his Hillbilly Elegy aligned properly with the firm's Rise of the Rest ideology.
Case quickly hired Vance and brought him on board. He hired Vance when he was still working on Peter Thiel's Mithril firm.

In December 2017, Vance and Case launched the first Rise of the Rest Seed Fund. It was a huge success as they raised $150 million from investors with billionaires like Jeff Bezos, Tory Burch, Ray Dalio, John Doerr, and several others all investing. Armed with this capital, the firm proceeded to make their first investments in several companies including investing in Branch Insurance, and FreightWaves.

Vance worked with Steve Case at Revolution for about a year and six months.

After Vance left the firm, he considered diving into politics but then decided to focus on his young family.

Narya Capital

In 2020, he launched his own venture capital firm, Narya Capital, raising more than $93 million from notable backers, including Thiel and other influential investors. Narya Capital focused on a diverse range of investments, reflecting Vance's ongoing commitment to supporting innovative companies across various industries.

Narya Capital positions itself as a nimble and inquisitive investment firm, dedicated to supporting founders who are addressing some of society's most pressing challenges. According to the company's website, the firm is backing a range of innovative companies that are making significant strides in various sectors, including:

- Healthcare Accessibility: Narya-backed initiatives are working to make Medicare more understandable and actionable for eligible citizens, ensuring that vital healthcare resources are accessible to those who need them most.
- Sustainable Agriculture: The firm is investing in methods that promote the growth of fruits and vegetables locally, aiming to provide fresher, healthier, and more affordable food options for families across the nation.

- Advanced Therapies: Narya is supporting companies that leverage advanced therapies to combat the rising prevalence of obesity, diabetes, cardiovascular diseases, and cancer, addressing critical public health concerns.
- Defense Technology: The firm is focused on protecting national assets through the development of advanced defense technologies, enhancing the security of the nation.
- Life Sciences Manufacturing: Narya is committed to on-shoring essential pre-clinical, clinical, and manufacturing capabilities for cutting-edge life sciences companies, promoting innovation within the industry.
- Affordable Insurance: By harnessing technology, Narya is working to make car and home insurance more affordable for consumers, aiming to ease financial burdens on families.
- Democratic Values: The firm is dedicated to defending the pillars of democracy, including free speech and capitalism, ensuring that these foundational principles remain strong in the face of challenges.

However, Narya Capital faced cancellation of its business charter in Delaware due to clerical oversights, specifically the resignation of its registered agent, Cogency Global. This administrative error led to the state changing Narya's status to "canceled," although the firm continued its operations, including significant investments in companies like Rumble and Kriya Therapeutics.

After reconciling with Delaware and paying an administrative fine, Narya regained its good standing. Legal experts described the oversight as a basic error in corporate governance, which could potentially deter future investments due to perceived incompetence. Despite this lapse, experts noted that such cancellations are common and typically do not materially affect a company's operations.

Despite these challenges, Narya Capital appears to still be operational, having registered a new entity shortly after the cancellation.

Vance in the Senate

J.D. Vance has been serving as the junior United States senator from Ohio since January 3, 2023. His ascent to the Senate is notable not only for his personal journey from a working-class background to political office but also for the significant ideological shifts and controversies that have characterized his tenure. Vance's political career has been shaped by his experiences as an author, venture capitalist, and commentator, leading to his election to the Senate after a successful campaign in the 2022 midterm elections.

Election to the Senate

In 2021, he declared his desire to run for the U.S. Senate seat being vacated by retiring Republican Senator Rob Portman. His campaign was bolstered by substantial financial support from prominent figures in the Republican Party, including Peter Thiel, who donated a total of $15 million to Vance's 2022 campaign to a super Political Action Committee(PAC) supporting Vance's candidacy.

Peter Thiel helped Vance in several ways in his senatorial campaign. Aside from the donations he made, he also helped him find favor in Trump's eyes because before this, Vance was very critical of

Trump. He had called Trump several names and even likened him to Hitler.

However, Vance's mentor, Peter Thiel, was in good standing with Donald Trump; he had even donated $1.5 million to sponsor pro-Trump outfit during the 2016 election. Even though Trump was not in office during this senatorial election, he still had the loyalty of many Republicans. According to a report from the New York Times, Thiel took Vance to go meet Trump at his palm beach home in Mar-a-Lago in 2021. Thiel helped the duo reconcile their differences.

Vance's campaign then emphasized his alignment with Trumpism– the political ideologies of Donald Trump, who endorsed him about a month before the election, helping him secure the Republican primary with 32% of the vote against several challengers. He went on to defeat Democratic nominee Tim Ryan in the general election, receiving 53% of the vote.

Legislative Priorities and Committee Assignments

Upon taking office, Vance became a member of the 118th United States Congress. His committee assignments include the Senate Committee on

Banking, Housing, and Urban Affairs, the Senate Committee on Commerce, Science, and Transportation, and the Senate Special Committee on Aging. These assignments reflect his focus on economic issues, infrastructure, and the well-being of older Americans.

Vance's legislative priorities have been influenced by his background and the needs of his constituents in Ohio. He has positioned himself as a strong advocate for conservative policies, particularly those aimed at addressing the economic challenges faced by working-class families. One of his notable actions in the Senate included co-sponsoring a bipartisan bill with Senator Raphael Warnock (D-GA) to lower the price of insulin, demonstrating his willingness to work across party lines on issues affecting healthcare affordability.

Additionally, Vance collaborated with Senator Elizabeth Warren (D-MA) on legislation aimed at holding executives accountable when large banks fail, reflecting his commitment to financial oversight and consumer protection. This willingness to engage in bipartisan efforts has been somewhat atypical for a senator closely aligned with the more extreme elements of the Republican Party.

Controversies and Criticisms

Despite his bipartisan efforts, Vance's tenure has not been without controversy. He faced criticism for his delayed response to the 2023 train derailment in East Palestine, Ohio, which resulted in a significant environmental disaster.

A Norfolk Southern freight train derailed, resulting in 38 cars going off the tracks, several of which were carrying hazardous materials, including vinyl chloride. This chemical is known for its potential health risks, including cancer. The derailment led to a massive fire that burned for over two days, prompting the evacuation of residents within a one-mile radius due to safety concerns about air quality and potential exposure to toxic substances.

Vance's office released an official statement ten days after the derailment, leading to accusations of negligence and a lack of urgency in addressing the concerns of affected residents.

Vance's initial social media response was perceived as insufficient, prompting backlash from both constituents and political opponents.

In the aftermath of the derailment, Vance authored an op-ed in *The Washington Post*, advocating for financial assistance to those impacted by the disaster, similar to the Paycheck Protection Program (PPP) funds provided during the COVID-19 pandemic. This stance drew criticism from some within his party, who felt that it contradicted the traditional Republican approach to disaster relief and government intervention.

Vance Against Donald Trump

In the pages above, we have discussed slightly on Vance's opposition to Trump, but here we would explore it more.

J.D. Vance's political journey is marked by a significant evolution in his relationship with Donald Trump, transitioning from a vocal critic to a staunch supporter. This shift reflects not only Vance's personal political ambitions but also the broader dynamics within the Republican Party as it has increasingly embraced populist and nationalist themes.

Early Opposition to Trump

During the 2016 presidential campaign, Vance was openly critical of Donald Trump. In a July 2016 article for *The Atlantic*, he described Trump as "cultural heroin," suggesting that the former reality television star and businessman was offering easy solutions to complex social problems without addressing the root causes of issues facing the working class.

Vance expressed concern that Trump's rhetoric and approach could lead the white working class to a "very dark place." His comments during this period positioned him firmly within the "Never Trump" camp, a group of Republicans who opposed Trump's candidacy on ideological grounds.

In interviews, Vance articulated his discomfort with Trump's style and substance. He told NPR's Terry Gross that he found it hard to "stomach" Trump, emphasizing that he believed Trump's approach was detrimental to the working-class communities he sought to represent.

In an October 2016 interview with Charlie Rose, Vance reiterated his position by stating, "I'm a 'Never Trump' guy. I never liked him." This clear opposition to Trump during the campaign was indicative of Vance's initial alignment with more traditional Republican values, which emphasized decorum and policy over the populist rhetoric that Trump championed.

The Shift in Stance

Vance's relationship with Trump began to change as he entered the political arena himself. In 2021, he announced his candidacy for the U.S. Senate seat being vacated by Rob Portman. As he prepared for his campaign, Vance recognized the necessity of aligning himself with Trump's base to secure support within the Republican Party. The political landscape had shifted significantly since 2016, with Trump's influence over the party growing stronger and more pervasive.

During his Senate campaign, Vance adopted many of Trump's talking points and positions, emphasizing themes of nationalism and populism that resonated with voters in the Rust Belt, where he had grown up. He began to embrace Trump's rhetoric on immigration, trade, and foreign policy, positioning himself as a candidate who understood the concerns of working-class voters. This strategic pivot was crucial for Vance, as it allowed him to tap into the fervent support that Trump commanded among Republican primary voters.

Embracing Trump's Policies

Once elected to the Senate, Vance continued to align himself closely with Trump and the populist elements of the Republican Party. He frequently echoed Trump's themes in his speeches and public appearances, advocating for an "America First" approach to domestic and foreign policy.

Vance's Senate tenure has been characterized by a focus on issues that resonate with the working class, including economic revitalization, healthcare affordability, and a skepticism towards traditional

Republican positions on free trade and military intervention.

Vance's alignment with Trump also extended to social issues, where he adopted conservative stances on topics such as abortion, gender identity, and immigration. He has been a vocal opponent of gender-affirming care for minors, co-sponsoring legislation that would criminalize such practices. His positions on these issues reflect the broader ideological shift within the Republican Party towards a more aggressive and confrontational stance on cultural matters.

Vance and Project 2025

Even though Trump has openly distanced himself from Project 2025 stating that he had no idea who is behind the project, it is known that more than one hundred people who served in his administration during his time as the president helped in crafting the policy proposals of Project 2025. Trump called some of the proposals "ridiculous and abysmal," stating he has "nothing to do with them."

On the flipside, Vance is open about his association with the leaders of Heritage Foundation, the organization behind Project 2025.

Kevin Roberts, the president of the Heritage Foundation has close ties with Vance. He had openly shared his own reason why Trump should pick Vance as his running mate stating that he was a man who embodies hope for the future of the United States.

Additionally, in an article reported by Politico in March of 2024, Roberts also reiterated his support of Vance stating that Vance would be "one of the leaders, if not the leader" of Project 2025 movement. To show their close ties, the foreword of Roberts' new book *Dawn's Early Light: Taking*

Back Washington to Save America, which will be released on September 24, 2024 was written by Vance.

In the editorial review of the book he wrote, something like— *This is the first time a figure of Roberts's prominence and standing within the American conservative movement has attempted to outline a truly novel vision for the future of conservatism... We are now collectively recognizing that it is time to rally our forces and prepare for the battles ahead. In the conflicts that lie ahead, these ideas represent a crucial weapon.*

To be clear, Vance has not openly given his 100 percent support to the policy proposals of Project 2025 aside from saying that the project contains some "good ideas," but that there are some that he disagrees with.

So, Vance's dealings with the folks at Project 2025 really show how tightly he's woven into the big-picture goals of the right-wing populist crowd within the Republican Party. Now that he's in the Senate and even on the ticket as Trump's VP pick, his work with Project 2025 is his way of showing he's all in on transforming how the federal government works and pushing forward those conservative policies that the party's die-hard supporters really go for.

But here's the thing—Project 2025 has its fair share of drama and controversy. Because of that, we're sort of on hold about where Vance really stands on everything to do with this project until after the votes are counted. We'll just have to wait and see how deep his commitment goes once the election dust settles.

Understanding Project 2025

Project 2025 is like the Heritage Foundation's game plan for getting ready in case there's a Republican lead at the helm in 2025. They're piecing together a whole policy playbook dealing with the big ticket items: the economy, immigration, schools, and how we interact with the world.

The idea is all about leaning into a conservative style of running things—think smaller government, endorsing free markets, and a nod to traditional values. This project isn't just spinning its wheels; it's quite a big deal because it reflects how the Republican Party is sort of reshaping itself lately.

They've been tapping into a more populist vibe lately, really trying to speak to the everyday folks.

Project 2025 is there to channel that energy and make sure it translates into solid, conservative policy actions if they get the chance to call the shots federally.

Vance's Alignment with Project 2025

J.D. Vance is really flying the flag for Trump's style of politics, so it makes total sense he's getting behind Project 2025. He's all in because it matches up with his push for right-wing populism. You know, the kind that puts regular folks first before the big shots and old-school institutions. Vance isn't just talking; he's been there. Growing up in a hard-hit Ohio town, he knows what it's like for the working class, and he champions their cause.

Vance isn't shy about shaking things up either. He's been pushing hard for a big change within Project 2025 - particularly, he wants to shake up the federal workforce. He thinks a lot of the career bureaucrats should be replaced by folks who are in tune with the administration's goals. He even said on a podcast back in 2021 that if he could whisper a word of advice to Donald Trump, it'd be to fire every mid-level bureaucrat and swap them with loyalists ready to roll up their sleeves and get to work on their agenda.

So, not too long ago in a February 2023 interview on ABC News, J.D. Vance doubled down on his ideas. He said he wants to switch out those mid-level bureaucrats with folks who really get what the administration is trying to do. That's right in line with what Project 2025 is all about—transforming the federal government by getting rid of career officials who might slow down their conservative plans, and bringing in appointees who are all in on executing the administration's top priorities.

Vance has been a staunch supporter of this shake-up well before anyone talked about him as Trump's possible sidekick for the 2024 run. It just goes to show how devoted he is to the Project 2025 blueprint, and how ready he is to take bold steps to reshape the federal workforce to align with the goals of the MAGA crowd.

And with Vance's recent nod as Trump's running mate for the 2024 election, it's clear how much populism is steering the Republican Party these days. His backing of Project 2025 fits snugly with his wider political vision—like pushing for policies that give American workers a leg up, trimming down excessive government, and sticking up for traditional values.

Key Policy Areas

Project 2025 really covers a lot of ground, hitting on a bunch of issues that J.D. Vance cares deeply about too. At the heart of it, there's a big push to fix up the federal workforce—a cause Vance has been vocal about ever since he entered the Senate. He's pretty outspoken about what he sees as a bloated, sluggish federal bureaucracy and wants to see it leaner and more accountable.

Beyond just cutting down inefficiencies in government jobs, Project 2025 also dives into education, healthcare, and immigration—all hot topics for Vance. He's not shy about his take on higher education either, calling out universities for being too left-leaning and pushing for changes that would bring more conservative values into the academic mix. His cheers for Project 2025's education plans show he's all for the federal government stepping up to steer the educational scene more conservatively.

Then there's healthcare—another biggie for Vance and Project 2025. He's been in the trenches, like with his support for legislation to cut insulin costs, and is all about making healthcare more affordable for regular families. This fits perfectly with Project 2025's wider aim to offer conservative solutions that make a real difference in everyday Americans' lives.

Criticism and Controversy

Even though Vance's political ideologies are aligned with Project 2025, not everyone's giving him a thumbs up for it.

Some critiquers worry that by pushing to trim down the government and boost free-market ideas, Project 2025 might skip over the real problems that the working class faces every day. They argue that Vance backing this initiative might just end up helping the rich get richer while leaving folks in less-privileged communities behind.

Also, let's not forget, Vance wasn't always a Trump cheerleader. Initially, he was quite critical of Trump and didn't support his run for president, which has some people wondering about his flip to full-on support now.

Even though Vance has pretty much wrapped himself in Trump's policies and talking points lately, there are still some doubters who aren't totally convinced about his dedication to Project 2025's ideas. They see his sudden alignment more as a tactic to grab political power than a real change of heart.

The Future of Vance and Project 2025

As Vance gears up as Trump's right-hand man for the 2024 presidential run, his deep dive into Project 2025 is set to be a big player in crafting the campaign's vibes and policy direction. The initiative's whole conservative game plan lines up nicely with where Vance sees the Republican Party heading, putting him front and center in the tussle over what the party stands for.

If he makes it to office, getting behind Project 2025 could really shake things up in American politics. His backing hints at him gunning for a gutsy conservative approach that looks out for the working class and wants to toss out the old ways of doing things. This kind of approach could strike a chord with voters who are after some real changes and tired of business as usual in politics.

However, some of the radical policies contained in Project 2025 may end up hurting the Republican party. This is why Trump distanced himself from this project claiming he knew nothing about it. Vance on the other hand has taken a different stance, dining with the leaders of Project 2025 shows he is perfectly aligned with the policy proposals of the Heritage Foundation.

Vances Political Ideologies

In this section, we will examine some of the political ideologies of J.D. Vance. It is clear that Vance is outspoken and will actively express his views if the Republicans clutch the helm of power. He will not be the kind of vice president who watches the president run the country; he will be upfront with his own views.

Here are some of the strongest political ideologies of J.D Vance.

Economic Populism

Economic populism is all about looking out for the working class and often clashes with the big shots and the old-school institutions. It's there to shake up economic inequalities and push for policies that help everyday folks instead of the big companies or the super-rich.

J.D. Vance has really taken up the mantle for the often-overlooked men and women in America's heartland. In his 2016 book, he dives deep into the troubles faced by working-class white Americans in the Rust Belt. He argues that deals like the North American Free Trade Agreement (NAFTA) really knocked the wind out of American manufacturing, wiping out good jobs. According to Vance, these economic hits have led to serious social issues like drug addiction, family troubles, and a general sense of hopelessness in places like the Midwest and Appalachia.

When he ran for the U.S. Senate in Ohio, Vance promised to stand up for American workers and take on the 'cosmopolitan elite' who he feels have left these folks behind. He's talked about wanting to renegotiate trade agreements to safeguard American jobs, slap tariffs on Chinese imports, and cut down on U.S. reliance on Chinese factories. Vance is all about bringing critical supply chains back home to lessen risks and make sure the U.S. can produce vital stuff like semiconductors, drugs, and medical gear on its own turf.

In a way, Vance's take on economic populism mirrors former President Donald Trump's 'America First' approach. Like Trump, Vance thinks the Republican Party needs a shift—away from its old free-market playbook towards a more nationalist, protectionist stance. He's even called out the GOP's top donors for, in his view, putting big business interests over the needs of working families.

Isolationism and Skepticism of Foreign Intervention

Vance has this approach where he mixes his economic populism with a real hesitancy about getting involved in other countries' battles. He thinks the U.S. should be less about policing the world and more about sorting out our own issues first.

After Russia went into Ukraine in February 2022, Vance became pretty vocal in the Republican Party about why America shouldn't go all in. He's worried we don't have enough gear or resources to help Ukraine and keep China in check at the same time. Vance figures we should really be keeping an eye on China, believing they're a bigger deal for the future of America.

He doesn't just stop with Ukraine, though. Vance hasn't been a fan of the U.S. helping Saudi Arabia in Yemen, and he's even questioned whether being in NATO is worth it. Plus, he kind of looks up to Hungary's Prime Minister Viktor Orbán, who's all about tightening the reins of power.

Overall, he's pretty skeptical when it comes to the U.S. jumping into international conflicts. Vance doesn't think we should get involved unless it's truly necessary for our security. He's also quite critical of how America's efforts to reshape countries like Afghanistan and Iraq turned out, seeing them as expensive letdowns.

Authoritarian Tendencies

Vance's ideas on keeping the U.S. out of foreign entanglements mix with what some might call a penchant for tough-guy leadership styles back home. He's really into some tough rulers who like to keep all the political power up top.

In an interview back in 2021, Vance threw out that if Trump got another go at the presidency, he should maybe shake up the government by firing folks who aren't on board and replacing them with his own people—even if that meant bending the rules a bit. Vance thinks the folks running the show in Washington have gotten too mighty, and it might be time for some drastic moves to dial that back.

Vance sure seems to think our political system's got some serious cracks that need a major fix. He's been pretty outspoken against what he calls the 'deep state,' accusing longtime government workers of tripping up Trump's plans. He's all in on this 'national conservative' idea too, which is about steering the government to uphold traditional values and stand up to what he sees as liberal overreach.

But not everyone's a fan. Critics say Vance is playing with fire, edging toward authoritarianism and stomping on democratic principles. They bring up his cheers for Orbán, the Hungarian leader who's tightened his grip by tweaking the constitution, squeezing the press, and grabbing more control over various institutions. Vance also digs the thoughts of Patrick Deneen, a thinker who's pretty much given up on liberalism and wants to return to a society rooted in old-school traditions and community vibes.

Christian Nationalism

Vance blends his politics with a strong dose of Christian nationalism, advocating for the idea that America should embrace its Christian roots. He often says that the U.S. was built on Judeo-Christian values and that these are central to the nation's identity.

During a speech in 2022, Vance shared how his faith drives his support for Israel. He explained, "A lot of us here believe that our savior Jesus was born, lived, and was resurrected in that small area along the Mediterranean, and that's significant for us." He believes U.S. foreign policy should consider Christians more heavily.

Vance champions policies supporting traditional families and moral values, reflecting his stance on Christian nationalism. He's openly critical of the LGBTQ+ rights movement and stresses the need for stronger support for families and greater incentives for having children. Vance also draws inspiration from Sohrab Ahmari, who promotes a vision of politics that does away with the separation of church and state.

However, Vance faces criticism for possibly weaponizing his Christian beliefs for political ends and promoting an America that might exclude non-Christians and secular people. Critics argue that his views conflict with the foundational American principles of religious freedom and diversity.

Vance's Stance on Abortion and Reproductive Rights

J.D. Vance's take on abortion and reproductive rights really stands out in his political portfolio, especially as he's become a key figure in the Republican Party. His opinions here aren't just personal; they're intertwined with his political tactics and his nod to the broader conservative agenda. This stance became particularly relevant following the Supreme Court's overturning of Roe v. Wade in the Dobbs v. Jackson Women's Health Organization case.

A bit of background: Roe v. Wade was a pivotal 1973 Supreme Court decision that declared a nationwide right to abortion, centering around a case where "Jane Roe" — who was later revealed as Norma McCorvey — challenged Texas laws that banned abortion. The Court, with a 7-2 vote, decided that a woman's right to choose was protected under the privacy rights guaranteed by the 14th Amendment.

That decision had been at the heart of a heated national dialogue on abortion. Many opponents hoped to reverse it, arguing that it was incorrectly decided and that the Constitution didn't safeguard abortion rights. Their moment came in June 2022 when the Supreme Court, in Dobbs v. Jackson Women's Health Organization, nixed Roe v. Wade, erasing the federal right to abortion and letting states make their own rules about it. This shift led several states to either ban or heavily limit abortion, marking a massive win for those against abortion rights and a big blow for its advocates.

In light of these changes, Vance has really leaned into being a major voice for tightening abortion regulations.

Vance's Position on Abortion

Vance truly believes that every life starts right from conception—that little heartbeat—and feels that these early lives deserve rights and protection just like anyone else. That's why he's been all-in with pushing for laws that make it tougher to get an abortion, standing strong with the pro-life folks and sticking to what the Republican Party thinks about all this. During his run for the U.S. Senate, he often talked about his commitment to the unborn, pushing the idea of a society that really values and cherishes life.

He's also come out praising some of the really tough abortion laws out there, like the one in Texas—Senate Bill 8. It basically stops most abortions after six weeks of pregnancy. Vance sees this law as a protector of unborn kids and believes it's a critical step towards what he sees as true justice and respect for life, even aligning himself with some of the more hardline views within the anti-abortion crowd.

Vance's take on abortion really strikes a chord with a lot of conservative folks, especially in places like Ohio where there's a strong push for pro-life policies.

He's pretty much on the same page as Project 2025, which spells out a tough stance on abortion. They want to pull out all the stops using what the government can already do to cut down on abortion access. This even includes dusting off the old Comstock Act—yeah, that's a law from way back in 1873. Originally, it was all about keeping what was considered 'obscene' materials out of the mail, which back then meant anything to do with contraceptives or abortion.

So, this law, named after Congressman Anthony Comstock, basically said you couldn't send anything considered 'obscene, lewd, or lascivious' through the mail, and yes, that included anything about sexual health, contraception, or abortion.

Since he stepped into his role as a U.S. senator, Vance has really rolled up his sleeves to push his anti-abortion agenda forward. He's been busy co-sponsoring bills that make it harder to get an abortion, and he's all about cutting off funding to places that provide abortion services. It's clear he's serious about supporting pro-life policies and fits right in with the larger Republican game plan to dial back reproductive rights.

A big focus for Vance has been on tightening the rules around access to abortion pills, especially after the big Dobbs court decision. He's really throwing his weight behind making sure those laws are enforced.

Vance has made it pretty clear that he thinks the federal government should step up its game in enforcing the laws that are already on the books against distributing stuff related to abortions. This lines up pretty neatly with what Project 2025 is shooting for. Of course, this stance hasn't gone over well with everyone—reproductive rights advocates, in particular, are up in arms. They say these kinds of moves would just make it even tougher for women to get essential healthcare services they need.

Criticism and Controversy

Vance's views on abortion definitely stir up quite the debate. Critics say he's pretty out of step with what most Americans think, since a lot of people do support at least some access to abortion services.

Polls keep showing that a good chunk of folks believe in keeping the option open, especially in really tough situations like rape, incest, or when the mom's health is on the line. But Vance's firm stand against abortion has really ruffled the feathers of reproductive rights advocates. They see his views as a part of this bigger pattern of pretty extreme stances within the Republican Party.

There's quite a stir because Vance mentioned using the Comstock Act to block access to abortion pills. People who support women's rights are really worried about it. They say using this old law to restrict reproductive healthcare feels a bit authoritarian, like it's erasing women's freedom to make their own health decisions. It's making some folks accuse Vance and others who think like him of ignoring what most people want and just pushing their own views on everyone.

Vance's Political Strategy

Vance's stance on abortion really looks like a calculated play given his political goals. As he gears up for the 2024 presidential run alongside Donald Trump, coming out strong for the pro-life cause is key to winning over conservative voters.

The Republican Party has been really hammering on this as a major issue, and by Vance staking his ground here, he's proving himself a faithful player to the base. He's definitely trying to rally the evangelical Christians and other conservative folks who see this issue as top priority. Sticking close to the pro-life label could help boost his image in the party, plus it sets him apart from other moderates who might be treading a softer line on abortion rights.

Vance On No-Fault Divorce

J.D. Vance really leans into traditional family values, and his take on no-fault divorce shows that. He thinks the easy-out option of modern divorces doesn't sit well with the idea of family that he champions.

It ties into his bigger story about how he feels society's slipping and how these shifting cultural tides are messing with family life, especially in working-class communities.

The Concept of No-Fault Divorce

You know, back in the 70s, they came up with these no-fault divorce laws. The idea was to make splitting up easier and less of a nasty legal battle for everyone involved. But some folks, like J.D. Vance, think these laws have actually done more harm than good.

Vance believes that the ease of getting a divorce these days has changed how we view marriage. Instead of seeing it as a lifelong commitment, he reckons people now treat it like a relationship that's easy to just toss aside when the going gets tough. And he's worried that this mindset is hurting kids and families.

In Vance's eyes, the rise in divorce rates is directly linked to the introduction of no-fault divorce laws. He feels these laws have devalued marriage as an institution and made it too simple to walk away from your spouse without any real consequences.

Now, I'm not saying I agree or disagree with Vance's stance. But it's clear he's passionate about this issue and sees it as a major factor in the breakdown of traditional family structures in America today. He's not afraid to voice his concerns and push for changes to the current divorce system.

Cultural Critique of Divorce

When Vance talks about divorce, he often brings up what he sees as a decline in our culture. He believes that the sexual revolution and the rise of no-fault divorce have really shaken up traditional family values. According to him, the idea that people can just walk away from unhappy marriages hasn't actually made anyone happier. Instead, it's created a lot of emotional and social chaos, especially for kids.

Vance is pretty skeptical about the idea that ending a bad marriage is always a good thing. In a video he made for high school students, he pointed out that in the past, many couples stuck it out through tough times for the sake of keeping the family together. He even shared stories about his grandparents, who had a rocky relationship but stayed married until they passed away. He uses their story to make his point that sticking with a marriage, even when things get tough, is something we should value.

Vance believes that kids from divorced families often deal with a lot of emotional and psychological struggles that can really impact how they grow up and form relationships later on.

He's pushing for a rethink of divorce laws because he wants to encourage a culture that sees marriage as a lifelong commitment. Vance thinks that making it harder to get divorced might motivate couples to tackle their problems instead of just splitting up at the first sign of trouble. This view fits into a larger conservative belief that traditional family structures are crucial for a healthy society.

Political Context and Support

Vance isn't the only conservative politician who's against no-fault divorce. Folks like Tom Cotton and Mike Johnson have also been speaking out about this issue, arguing that it's all about protecting the importance of marriage.

Now, Vance hasn't actually put forward any bills to get rid of no-fault divorce, but he's definitely trying to sway people's opinions on it. He's part of a faction in the Republican Party that thinks America's moral and cultural foundations are crumbling. Their fix? Emphasizing traditional family values, faith, and going back to the way things used to be.

These conservatives believe that making divorce harder will encourage couples to work through their problems instead of just calling it quits at the first sign of trouble. They see no-fault divorce as a symptom of a society that doesn't value marriage and family like it used to.

So while Vance may not have a specific plan to change the divorce laws, he's definitely using his platform to push this idea that we need to rethink our attitudes about marriage and commitment. He's tapping into a broader conservative movement that wants to reshape the cultural conversation around these issues.

Criticism and Controversy

Vance's stance on no-fault divorce has sparked a fair amount of criticism. Many people argue that he overlooks the complexities of individual situations, especially when it comes to cases involving domestic abuse or couples who just can't get along anymore. Critics say that making it necessary to prove wrongdoing in divorce could keep victims stuck in harmful relationships, putting their safety and independence at risk.

On top of that, some folks believe that Vance's views reflect a broader conservative trend of romanticizing the past without really considering the realities of modern relationships. They argue that having the option to leave an unhappy marriage is actually really important for people looking to improve their lives and well-being.

Vance on Same-Sex Marriages

J.D. Vance has quite a few thoughts on the same-sex marriage movement and LGBTQ+ rights, aligning closely with core conservative principles. He's spoken about his stance as a way to protect what he sees as essential societal norms.

He's leveled some critiques at the LGBTQ+ rights movement, claiming that it challenges traditional family setups. Vance argues that efforts to support same-sex marriage and expand LGBTQ+ rights stray from the values he thinks should shape American culture.

He's also been vocal about his worries that these movements force their views on others, especially in schools where he's concerned about the presence of LGBTQ+ topics in educational content.

In an interview back in 2021, Vance shared his view that LGBTQ+ rights shouldn't overshadow parental rights and old-school values. He really pushes for parents to have control over their kids' education, especially when it comes to gender and sexuality topics. This opinion lines up with a wider conservative worry that LGBTQ+ ideas are too present in public life.

Also, Vance hasn't held back on his thoughts about the legal and cultural effects of the Obergefell v. Hodges case, which made same-sex marriage legal across the U.S. in 2015. He's worried that the decision has sidelined those with traditional marriage views, seeing it as a risk to religious freedom and the rights of those who disagree with same-sex marriage for moral or religious reasons.

It looks like Vance really leans into a style that appeals to folks who believe traditional values are slipping away and who might feel overlooked by the more progressive trends. He presents himself as the champion of the working-class American, especially those who haven't vibed with the direction some social movements are heading.

His take on the LGBTQ+ rights, which he often critiques, slots right into his larger aim of getting conservative voters to band together in favor of old-school family values and religious beliefs. However, there are plenty of critics who say Vance's stance isn't just old-fashioned—it's actively harmful.

They argue that his views contribute to leaving LGBTQ+ people out in the cold, going against the more modern understanding of marriage and family dynamics. This push and pull is pretty reflective of the bigger conversation happening in the Republican Party and across the U ailg.ng.s. What's the right balance between sticking to traditional values and recognizing the rights of LGBTQ+ people? It's a tough one.

Vance on Gun Laws

J.D. Vance has stirred up some strong feelings with his political views, especially when he brushed off gun violence as "fake problems." That's a bold stance that has thrown him into the hot seat, especially given all the heated debates about gun control and public safety we're seeing across the United States.

When Vance spoke about gun issues, he was right in the thick of a larger discussion on what's troubling our society—this is all happening against the backdrop of terrifying mass shootings and the increase in gun violence. His comments popped up during a Republican primary campaign, a time when candidates are trying to figure out how to connect with their people without straying too far from what the party faithful, who typically aren't keen on strict gun laws, want to hear. It's a tricky line to walk, for sure.

In an interview in 2022, Vance threw out that we're kinda missing the mark with all this talk about gun control. He believes the core problems are more about society falling apart, mental health issues, and families breaking down, not just about how easy it is to get guns. He thinks this whole focus on guns is just a way for liberals to shift the spotlight away from these deeper, messier social issues. It's a pretty common view among certain conservative leaders who feel that gun control laws don't really get to the heart of why violence happens in the first place.

When Vance called gun issues "fake problems," it really ruffled feathers across the board—not just among gun control supporters and Democrats, but even some folks in his own party weren't too pleased. Critics were quick to point out that brushing off gun violence like that really overlooks the real pain and loss felt by victims and their families. They argued that it downplays the critical need to tackle the spate of mass shootings that's been haunting the nation.

Gun control advocates were quick to call out Vance's remarks as part of a bigger trend where lots of Republican lawmakers seem hesitant to really confront the harsh truths of gun violence. They argue that by labeling gun issues as mere distractions, Vance and some of his party pals are dodging their duty to act on laws that could curb this violence. This criticism hits hard especially because of how often mass shootings occur in the

United States, leading to devastating losses and sparking louder cries for tougher gun control.

Vance's Broader Political Strategy

Vance's take on gun violence isn't just about the issue itself; it's really tied into his whole political game plan and where he stands ideologically. As a Republican and a fan of Donald Trump, he's really trying to sync up with the party's core supporters. These folks hold the Second Amendment rights super close and aren't too fond of gun control. So, when Vance talks about gun violence the way he does, it's likely a move to connect with conservative voters who see owning a gun as a basic right and view any kind of restrictions as a hit to their personal freedom.

So, when Vance brushes off gun issues as "fake," it looks a lot like he's making a calculated move to win over right-wing supporters, especially in places like the Rust Belt where guns are a big part of the local culture. By standing against gun control and framing it as protecting individual rights against liberal policies, Vance is really playing up his role as a defender of conservative values.

A lot of Vance's views on guns are also shaped by his personal background. He often talks about his grandma, a key figure in his life, who was big on gun rights and taught him about responsible gun ownership. Growing up in a working-class area in Ohio, guns were more than just weapons; they were essential for protection and a symbol of self-reliance.

In his books and talks, Vance really hammers home the point that owning a gun is all about giving people, especially those in rural spots, a boost in empowerment. He believes that for a lot of folks, guns aren't just a right; they're essential for personal safety and having control over their own lives. His grandma, Mamaw, was a prime example of this belief. She didn't just own one, but several handguns. Vance often shares stories about how Mamaw really valued having those guns around.

During his speech on the third night of the 2024 Republican National Convention, Vance shared a personal story about his grandmother. He mentioned how his Mamaw passed away just before he deployed to Iraq in 2005. While sorting through her belongings, he discovered 19 loaded handguns hidden throughout her house—in places like under the bed, in her closet, and even in the silverware drawer. Vance and his family were initially puzzled by the find. But then it dawned on them—towards the end of her life, Mamaw wasn't getting around too well. The frail old lady made sure she was never too far from what she needed to protect her family, keeping a handgun within reach wherever she was in the house.

The Impact on Vance's Political Career

Vance's take on gun violence has been a bit of a double-edged sword for his political life. On one side, sticking close to the party's core views and taking a tough stance on gun issues has really won over conservative voters who hold the Second Amendment dear. This approach has played a big part in his success at the polls, especially during the Republican primary where he was up against several other candidates.

On the flip side, Vance's comments have also made him a target for criticism from moderates and independents who think he's missing the mark on the real issues with gun violence in America. In a political atmosphere where public safety is a major worry for a lot of voters, his tendency to downplay gun problems might push away potential supporters who really want to see some action on gun control.

Broader Implications for Gun Control Discourse

Vance's way of calling gun issues "fake problems" really throws more fuel on the fire in the national conversation about gun control and public safety. It's part of a wider pattern where some conservative politicians push back against tighter gun laws, claiming that these laws don't really get to the root of the violence problem.

This viewpoint has a big impact on how laws are shaped, making the gap even wider between those pushing for gun control and those standing firm on gun rights.

After every high-profile mass shooting, the debate around gun control really heats up, with advocates pushing hard for big reforms to tackle the crisis. Vance's comments shine a light on the tightrope lawmakers have to walk in dealing with this tricky issue, especially in a polarized political climate where opinions on gun rights and public safety are super entrenched.

Vance on Climate Change

Vance's stance on climate change has really shifted over time. He's been a bit skeptical about mainstream climate science and tends to focus more on economic issues, especially when it comes to how they impact the working-class folks back in Ohio. His views are pretty typical of a larger trend in the Republican Party, where climate change tends to take a backseat to economic growth and job creation.

Early Skepticism and Economic Focus

Vance is pretty skeptical about rushing into climate change policies, especially those that might shake up the economy. He's big on pushing economic development first, especially in areas like the Rust Belt that have been built on manufacturing and fossil fuels. His upbringing in a working-class neighborhood really shapes how he sees these issues. He tends to put job security and economic stability ahead of tough environmental rules.

Vance has often pointed out in his talks that climate change efforts could really hit working-class Americans hard, especially those in coal, oil, and manufacturing jobs. He's worried that trying to cut carbon emissions might trigger job cuts and economic downturns in areas that depend heavily on these industries. This angle really clicks with a lot of folks in Ohio, where the economy has been struggling for a while.

Vance isn't a fan of federal regulations aimed at tackling climate change, seeing them as a kind of overreach that could choke off economic growth. He tends to side with the fossil fuel industry, pushing for policies that ensure energy independence and keep traditional energy sources in the mix. His approach has made him a big advocate for deregulation, arguing that less government meddling in energy markets will spark innovation and boost the economy.

Vance really isn't on board with initiatives that push the U.S. to move away from fossil fuels. He argues that these kinds of measures might jack up energy prices and make us less secure in terms of energy. He's all for beefing up domestic production of oil and natural gas to help boost the economy and keep us energy independent. This stance goes down well with a lot of voters in Ohio, where energy production is a big deal for the local economy.

Climate Change and Political Strategy

Vance's take on climate change isn't just about the environment—it's also a strategic political move. As a Republican senator, he's lined up with the base of his party, which tends to be wary of climate change initiatives they see as too progressive or bad for the economy.

By painting climate policies as a threat to jobs and economic stability, he casts himself as the champion of the working class. This story really strikes a chord with a lot of his constituents.

Vance's stance on climate change really plays into his larger political persona. He's positioned himself as a kind of populist within the Republican Party, pushing for policies that he says put regular Americans first, ahead of elites and environmental activists.

This populist angle is especially key as we look toward the 2024 presidential election. How Vance lines up with Trump and tackles issues like climate change is going to be under the microscope as he tries to win over a wide range of voters.

Criticism and Controversy

Vance's stance on climate change has definitely stirred up some debate. Critics say his skepticism about climate science and his resistance to climate policies are getting in the way of tackling a huge global issue.

Environmental advocates are sounding the alarm, warning that not taking action now could lead to some scary outcomes for future generations—think more natural disasters, rising sea levels, and big upsets to ecosystems.

People who disagree with Vance's views on climate change often point to the wide agreement among scientists that human activity is a big factor in global warming. They believe that tackling climate change with thorough policies is crucial for protecting the environment and securing a sustainable future.

Some folks see Vance's labeling of climate initiatives as bad for the economy as a big oversight, missing the long-term gains that could come from investing in renewable energy and sustainable practices.

Vance's Legislative Actions

In the Senate, Vance has consistently shown his doubts about climate change policies through his actions. He's voted against bills that try to tackle climate change and has thrown his support behind boosting fossil fuel production.

His cozy relationship with the fossil chefs industry and his resistance to environmental regulations have really resonated with conservative voters who put economic growth ahead of environmental worries.

Vance's moves in the legislature really mirror a bigger pattern we see in the Republican Party, where climate change is often viewed more as a political issue than a scientific one. By sticking with the party's line on climate change, Vance has made himself a major figure in the ongoing conversation about what direction U.S. energy policy should take.

Vance on Arming Teachers

J.D. Vance's idea to arm teachers as a way to deal with gun violence really shows off his general approach to gun policy, where he really focuses on individual rights and isn't too keen on government meddling.

His position on this has been influenced by his own experiences, his political beliefs, and the common views within the Republican Party about gun rights and keeping people safe.

Context of Vance's Position

The idea of arming teachers really picked up steam after some heartbreaking school shootings, like the ones at Sandy Hook Elementary in 2012 and Marjory Stoneman Douglas High School in 2018.

Following these terrible events, lots of policymakers and advocates started throwing around different ideas to make schools safer, and one of the more controversial suggestions was to let teachers carry firearms while on school grounds.

Vance's backing for arming teachers fits right into a bigger picture within the Republican Party that really values Second Amendment rights and sees gun ownership as key to personal security. He believes that if trained educators could carry firearms, it might scare off potential shooters and bump up safety for both students and staff. This view comes from the idea that responsible gun ownership can add an extra layer of protection, especially in places considered to be vulnerable.

Legislative Advocacy and Public Statements

Throughout his time in the Senate, Vance has been a strong voice for policies that back the right to bear arms and encourage gun ownership among law-abiding folks. He sees arming teachers as a down-to-earth way to handle school shootings, suggesting that it gives educators the power to defend themselves and their students if things go south.

In his interviews and speeches, Vance really pushes the idea of personal responsibility and the belief that people should have the tools to protect themselves from dangers.

Vance's push to arm teachers has really split opinions. His supporters see it as a must-do step to make schools safer. On the other hand, critics argue that bringing guns into schools could actually make things more dangerous and complicated.

They point to studies that suggest having guns in schools doesn't really make them safer and might even increase the chances of accidental shootings or misuse of firearms.

Political Implications

Vance backing the idea of arming teachers isn't just a policy stance; it's a bold political move that aligns him with the more hardcore, gun-rights defenders within the Republican Party.

His position really clicks with those in the party who are super committed to Second Amendment rights and view any gun control as a threat to personal freedoms. This stance gives him a solid connection to that part of the party's base.

This stance is a pretty big deal for Vance's political path, especially as he aims to firm up his support among conservative voters. By pushing for both gun ownership and the arming of teachers, he's really positioning himself as a big-time supporter of individual rights and a guardian of traditional values.

This is super relevant for his vice presidential campaign with Donald Trump, since it syncs well with Trump's own pro-gun views and strikes a chord with the core of the party.

Criticism and Controversy

Even though Vance's stance on arming teachers has won him some backers, it's definitely stirred up some controversy. Critics say that his approach makes the whole complex issue of gun violence seem too simple and doesn't really get to the heart of what causes these tragic events.

They argue that by focusing on arming teachers, we're missing out on broader, more effective solutions that could actually cut down on gun violence—things like better mental health support, community intervention programs, and reasonable gun control measures.

After mass shootings, the conversation about whether to arm teachers really heats up and opinions get deeply divided. Those against the idea worry about the risks of bringing guns into schools.

They question whether teachers can get adequate training and what it means to have firearms around kids every day. Their main concern is that instead of making schools safer, arming teachers might actually cause more harm than good, leading to accidents and possibly making the situations they're meant to prevent even worse.

Vance Opposes Expanding Background Checks and Red Flag Laws

So, J.D. Vance isn't too keen on making it tougher for people to buy guns or putting those red flag laws into practice, and that tells you a lot about where he stands on the Second Amendment and gun rights in general.

Seems like he's right in line with a lot of folks in the Republican Party who really value their personal freedoms and are wary of the government stepping in too much.

J.D. Vance's opposition to expanding background checks and implementing red flag laws is a significant aspect of his political ideology.

A Bit About Vance's Thoughts on Guns

Over time, Vance's take on gun control has changed a bit. Back in 2018, he was all for red flag laws, supporting actions to take guns away from folks who might be dangerous. But fast-forward to his Senate run, and you'll hear him calling these laws a big distraction and saying no to new gun safety laws.

He brands himself as a big-time defender of Second Amendment rights during his campaign, arguing that stricter gun laws are just a way to chip away at individual freedoms. He's not buying the need for better background checks or red flag laws because, in his view, they miss the main issues driving gun violence and just give more power to the government.

Why Vance Thinks Background Checks Aren't the Answer

Vance believes that expanding background checks won't really stop gun violence. He thinks the real problem lies in deeper social and economic issues, particularly in cities. He's said things like, 'Violence in our country is much more about density than guns,' making the point that just limiting guns won't really cut down on violence.

His point is that people who follow the laws shouldn't have to go through tougher screenings to buy a gun because the current laws are already keeping guns out of the wrong hands. Vance talks a lot about personal responsibility and the rights we have to protect ourselves, a common thread you'll hear from many conservative leaders.

Opposition to Red Flag Laws

Vance really isn't a fan of red flag laws. Basically, these laws let courts take guns away from people temporarily if they seem like they could be a danger to themselves or others.

The idea is to stop violence before it happens, especially in cases where someone might be going through a mental health crisis or threatening to hurt themselves. Family members, the police, or anyone really concerned can ask a court to limit someone's access to their firearms for a while. But Vance sees a big problem with this.

He's worried that these laws might just be the beginning of the government getting too involved. He thinks it's a slippery slope—today, it's taking guns away for a bit, but what about tomorrow?

In an interview in 2022, he said he believes that these laws don't really get to the heart of gun violence issues. His exact words were, 'I think the red flag laws, in particular, they certainly are a slippery slope. They also don't solve the problem of gun violence.' Vance is concerned that instead of helping, these laws could end up just being misused to take guns away from people who follow the law, without really making anyone safer.

Vance's not too fond of the way the government sticks its nose into things, and you can see that attitude in how he talks about all sorts of issues, like how the government handled stuff during the COVID-19 pandemic.

He thinks we've all seen the government go too far sometimes. That worry about the government overreaching—well, that's a big reason he's against those red flag laws. He's concerned that giving the government the power to mess with personal matters, like taking someone's guns away temporarily, could just be the start of infringing on more of our freedoms.

Political Implications

Vance's take on gun control isn't just about what he believes personally—it's also a smart play in the world of Republican politics.

By pushing back against background checks and red flag laws, he's really making himself out to be a hero for Second Amendment rights, which definitely wins him points with gun owners and conservatives who really value their personal freedoms.

His way of talking about it all ties right into the bigger Republican story that paints gun control as a threat to personal freedom. Vance is all about standing up to the so-called 'gun grabbers,' setting himself up as the guy defending honest, law-abiding folks from government interference.

This strategy does a lot for him politically. It sets him apart from the more middle-of-the-road Republicans who might be okay with some gun control measures. By sticking to a tough stance, he's looking to lock in support from voters who are super serious about keeping their Second Amendment rights intact.

Criticism and Controversy

So, Vance's stance against making it tougher to buy guns and against red flag laws hasn't exactly been met with applause from everyone.

Gun control advocates and even some people in his own party think he's not really on the same page as what's actually happening with gun violence in the U.S. They believe that straightforward steps, like background checks, are pretty crucial to keep guns away from the wrong folks.

His critics also say he's missing the point on red flag laws, arguing that these laws could actually stop some terrible events, like mass shootings, before they happen. They think if the police could temporarily take away guns from people who seem really dangerous, it could actually save some lives.

And then there's the talk about Vance flipping his views. Some folks accuse him of just playing politics—pointing out that he was all for red flag rights before but now he's against them. They suggest his current stance might be more about winning over conservative voters than sticking to a true belief in Second Amendment rights.

Why Trump Picked Vance

Donald Trump picking J.D. Vance as his VP for the 2024 election shows he's really tuning into the shifting vibes within the Republican Party and wants to double down on his hard-right agenda. There are a few big reasons behind this choice:

Loyalty and Alignment with Trumpism

Vance's journey from being skeptical of Trump during the 2016 campaign to becoming one of his staunchest supporters really shows his loyalty to the ex-president.

He initially had doubts about Trump, but later fully embraced his style and policies, especially around the claims of a stolen election and the GOP's trajectory.

This turnaround scored him Trump's backing during his successful Senate run in Ohio in 2022, boosting his rep as a true Trump loyalist. By picking Vance as his running mate, Trump is doubling down on someone who truly reflects the MAGA movement ethos, making sure his administration would stick with the hard-right policies his base loves.

Vance's solid backing of Trump's more contentious stances, from defending the January 6 Capitol rioters to critiquing the Biden administration, shows he's all in, standing firm as an ally who's unlikely to buck Trump's lead.

Appeal to the Working Class

Vance's roots as a working-class guy from Ohio really strike a chord with Trump's main supporters. His book, "Hillbilly Elegy," puts a spotlight on the struggles of the working class, especially in the Rust Belt—a key area for Trump's election plans. Vance's story of overcoming tough times and serving in the military after 9/11 helps paint him as a down-to-earth candidate who gets what regular Americans are going through.

By choosing Vance, Trump is showing he's focused on the concerns of working-class voters, especially those who feel overlooked by the usual political crowd. Vance's emphasis on economic issues, trade, and the feeling of being left out fits perfectly with Trump's approach, reinforcing the message that the GOP is the party for the working class.

Generational Shift and Energy

At 39, Vance brings a fresh face to Republican leadership. His youth and dynamic vibe might just draw in younger voters, a group that the GOP hasn't really nailed down yet. Trump picking Vance as his running mate is a clever move to inject some new energy into the campaign while still keeping the core supporters on board.

By choosing someone younger, Trump is looking to widen his appeal and make sure the party's message hits home with a varied crowd. Vance's knack for connecting with younger folks could really help the GOP make inroads with this increasingly important demographic, especially among non-college-educated young men, who've been leaning more Republican lately.

Foreign Policy Alignment

Vance's views on foreign policy really line up with Trump's "America First" mantra, which puts a strong focus on nationalism and a cautious take on getting involved in issues abroad. Vance has been pretty vocal about his doubts on the U.S.'s role in Ukraine and has suggested that it might be time to rethink America's international obligations. This kind of thinking marks a departure from the usual

Republican stance on foreign policy and tells voters that a Trump-Vance team would keep American interests front and center, steering clear of complex global issues. This approach is catching on within the party, with more voices calling for a less aggressive foreign policy.

Vance's take on these matters shows a bigger shift in the GOP towards a more populist angle. By picking Vance, Trump is doubling down on his goal to transform how the party handles foreign policy, aiming to attract voters who prefer to avoid military entanglements and focus more on domestic challenges.

Reinforcement of Trump's Message

Trump picking Vance really doubles down on his core messages and political identity. Vance comes across as a younger, sharper version of Trump, someone who can really sell the former president's ideas while staying true to his agenda.

This selection shows Trump's savvy in keeping a unified message in today's divided political scene, where voters really crave clear positions from their candidates.

By bringing Vance on board, Trump is looking to lock in his influence within the Republican Party and keep his policies and style at the forefront of political chatter. Vance, as a voice for the MAGA movement, is set to play a big role in steering the party's future and keeping its message consistent.

Vance Had the Backing of Influential People

Recall how Peter Thiel funded Trump's campaign in 2016, and how he helped Vance and Trump resolve their differences before he funded Vance's senatorial campaign.

Donald Trump's choice of J.D. Vance as his running mate can be seen as influenced by the backing of influential billionaires like Peter Thiel and other influential people. These wealthy figures have played a significant role in shaping the political landscape within the Republican Party, particularly in the context of right-wing populism and the alignment of economic interests with political agendas.

Peter Thiel has been known for his support of candidates who align with his libertarian and populist views. His backing can provide substantial financial and strategic resources to candidates like Vance, who advocate for a transformation of the federal government and a focus on issues that matter to working-class Americans.

Vance and His Family

The story of J.D Vance will not be complete without his wife, Usha Chilukuri.

J.D. Vance met his wife while they were both students at Yale Law School. Usha, born to Indian immigrants, grew up in the San Francisco area and has established herself as a successful litigator.

The couple married in 2014 in an interfaith ceremony that blended their diverse backgrounds—Vance being Christian and Usha Hindu. This union reflects Vance's belief in the importance of family, as they have created a home that embraces both of their cultural heritages.

Usha has been a supportive partner throughout Vance's political career, often accompanying him at public events and engaging in discussions about their family life. The couple emphasizes the importance of open communication and shared values in raising their children, navigating the complexities of their interfaith marriage while instilling a sense of identity in their kids.

Vance and Usha Vance are proud parents to three children: Ewan, Vivek, and Mirabel.

The End

The story of J.D Vance is an inspiring story of a man who came from nothing. He stood on the shoulders of giants like Peter Thiel to achieve greatness.

"Success is not just about individual effort; it's about standing on the shoulders of giants who pave the way for us."__ M.P Kruger(author).

About the Author

M.P. Kruger is a political analyst and author known for his insightful commentary on contemporary American politics, particularly the rise of populism within the Republican Party.

With a background in political science and a keen interest in the intersection of economics and governance, Kruger has dedicated his career to exploring the narratives that shape political identities in the United States.

In his latest book, "The Incredible Story of J.D. Vance: From Hillbilly Elegy to Political Power," Kruger delves into Vance's remarkable journey from a challenging upbringing in Ohio to becoming a prominent voice in the GOP.

Made in the USA
Monee, IL
02 August 2024

63143780R00062